Introduction

Personal finance and budgeting are crucial aspects of life that affect the financial stability and well-being of an individual. With the increasing cost of living and the uncertain economic climate, it's more important than ever to understand how to manage your finances and create a budget that works for you. This book is designed to provide you with the tools and information you need to take control of your finances, eliminate debt, and achieve your financial goals.

TABLE OF CONTENTS

Personal finance and budgeting are ongoing journeys, not one-time events. It's important to regularly review your financial situation and make adjustments as needed to ensure that you're on track to reach your goals. This book provides a solid foundation for your personal finance journey, but it's up to you to take the next steps and make the necessary changes to improve your financial well-being. Remember, the earlier you start and the more consistent you are, the more likely you are to achieve financial success. So keep learning, keep growing, and keep reaching for your financial dreams.

Chapter I: Understanding Personal Finance

In this chapter, we'll explore the basics of personal finance and why it's important to understand and manage your finances. Personal finance is the process of managing your money to achieve financial stability, security, and independence. It involves understanding your income, expenses, assets, and liabilities and making smart financial decisions to achieve your goals. Personal finance is important because it affects every aspect of your life. It determines your ability to pay bills, save for the future, and live comfortably. It also affects your financial security, your ability to handle unexpected expenses, and your ability to retire comfortably.

There are several key components of personal finance that you need to understand to effectively manage your finances. These include:

1. Income: Your income is the money you earn from your job, investments, or other sources. Understanding your income is the first step in managing your finances.

2. Expenses: Your expenses are the money you spend on living, such as food, housing, transportation, and other necessities. Understanding your expenses is critical to creating a budget and managing your finances.

3. Assets: Assets are things that you own that have value, such as your home, car, investments, and retirement accounts. Understanding your assets is important for creating a financial plan and reaching your goals.

4. Liabilities: Liabilities are things that you owe, such as credit card debt, student loans, and mortgages. Understanding your liabilities is important for managing debt and achieving financial stability.

By understanding these key components of personal finance, you'll be able to make informed decisions about your finances and achieve your financial goals. In the next chapter, we'll discuss the importance of setting financial goals and how to do so effectively.

Chapter II: Setting Financial Goals

In this chapter, we'll delve into the importance of setting financial goals and how to do so effectively. Setting financial goals is an essential part of personal finance because it provides direction and motivation for your financial journey. It gives you something to work towards and helps you stay focused on your priorities.

To set effective financial goals, you need to be specific, realistic, and measurable. Here are some steps to help you set financial goals:

1. Determine your priorities: What are your most important financial goals? Is it paying off debt, saving for a down payment on a house, or planning for retirement? Knowing your priorities will help you focus your efforts.

2. Make your goals specific: Instead of saying "I want to save money," specify how much money you want to save and by when. For example, "I want to save $10,000 for a down payment on a house by the end of the year."

3. Make your goals realistic: Your goals should be challenging but achievable. Don't set yourself up for failure by setting goals that are too ambitious.

4. Make your goals measurable: Establish a way to track your progress towards your goals. This could be as simple as tracking your savings in a spreadsheet or using a budgeting app.

5. Set short-term, medium-term, and long-term goals: Having a mix of short-term, medium-term, and long-term goals will help you stay motivated and focused. Short-term goals provide immediate gratification, medium-term goals keep you motivated, and long-term goals give you something to work towards for the future.

By following these steps, you'll be able to set effective financial goals that will help you achieve financial stability and success. In the next chapter, we'll discuss the process of creating a budget and how to make it work for you.

Chapter III: Creating a Budget

In this chapter, we'll explore the process of creating a budget and how to make it work for you. A budget is a financial plan that helps you manage your money by tracking your income and expenses. It allows you to see where your money is going and make adjustments as needed to reach your financial goals.

Here are some steps to help you create a budget:

1. Track your spending: Keep a record of all your expenses for at least a month to get a clear picture of where your money is going.
2. Categorize your expenses: Divide your expenses into categories such as housing, food, transportation, and entertainment.
3. Set spending limits: Based on your income and expenses, set limits for each category to ensure that you're not overspending.
4. Monitor your progress: Review your budget regularly to see where you can make adjustments and ensure that you're staying on track.
5. Make adjustments: If you find that you're overspending in a certain category, make adjustments to bring your spending back in line with your budget.

Creating a budget takes time and effort, but it's worth it in the long run. By creating a budget, you'll have a clear understanding of your finances, you'll be able to prioritize your spending, and you'll be able to reach your financial goals more easily. In the next chapter, we'll discuss the importance of saving and investing and how to do so effectively.

Chapter IV: Saving and Investing

In this chapter, we'll discuss the importance of saving and investing and how to do so effectively. Saving and investing are critical components of personal finance because they help you build wealth and achieve financial security.

Here are some steps to help you save and invest effectively:

1. Start small: Start by setting aside a small amount of money each month, even if it's just a few dollars. As you become more comfortable with saving, you can increase the amount.
2. Make saving automatic: Set up automatic transfers from your checking account to your savings account to make saving a habit.
3. Create an emergency fund: An emergency fund is a savings account that you use to cover unexpected expenses, such as medical bills or car repairs. Aim to save enough money to cover three to six months of living expenses.
4. Invest in a diversified portfolio: Investing in a mix of stocks, bonds, and other assets will help you minimize risk and maximize returns.
5. Seek professional advice: If you're not comfortable managing your investments on your own, consider seeking the advice of a financial advisor.

Saving and investing can be intimidating, but with the right approach and a little discipline, you can achieve financial stability and security. In the next chapter, we'll focus on managing debt and avoiding the pitfalls of overspending.

Chapter V:
Managing Debt

In this chapter, we'll explore the importance of managing debt and how to do so effectively. Debt can be a burden and can impact your financial well-being, so it's important to understand how to manage it effectively.

Here are some steps to help you manage debt:

1. Assess your debt: Make a list of all your debts, including the creditor, interest rate, and minimum monthly payment.
2. Prioritize your debts: Focus on paying off high-interest debt first, such as credit card debt, to minimize the amount of interest you pay over time.
3. Make a plan: Create a plan to pay off your debts, such as the debt snowball or debt avalanche method.
4. Stick to your plan: Consistency is key when it comes to paying off debt. Make your debt repayment a priority and stick to your plan.
5. Avoid overspending: Avoid adding to your debt by being mindful of your spending and avoiding overspending.

Managing debt can be a challenge, but with the right approach and a little discipline, you can become debt-free and improve your financial well-being. In the next chapter, we'll discuss the importance of protecting your finances and how to do so effectively.

Chapter VI: Protecting Your Finances

In this chapter, we'll focus on the importance of protecting your finances and how to do so effectively. Protecting your finances means taking steps to safeguard your money, assets, and personal information from theft, fraud, and other financial threats.

Here are some steps to help you protect your finances:

1. Secure your personal information: Keep your personal information, such as your Social Security number and bank account information, secure.
2. Use strong passwords: Use strong, unique passwords for all your financial accounts and change them regularly.
3. Monitor your accounts: Regularly review your bank and credit card statements to catch any unauthorized transactions.
4. Be cautious of scams: Be cautious of scams, such as phishing scams, and never give out personal information over the phone or online.
5. Purchase insurance: Consider purchasing insurance, such as life insurance, health insurance, and homeowner's insurance, to protect your finances and your loved ones.

Protecting your finances is an essential part of personal finance and requires due diligence and a little extra effort. By taking the steps outlined in this chapter, you'll be able to safeguard your finances and achieve financial stability and security. In the next chapter, we'll discuss the importance of staying on track and how to do so effectively.

Chapter VII:
Staying on Track

In this chapter, we'll focus on the importance of staying on track with your personal finance goals and how to do so effectively. Staying on track means consistently following your budget, saving and investing, and paying off debt, even when it's difficult.

Here are some steps to help you stay on track:

1. Review your progress regularly: Regularly review your budget and financial goals to ensure that you're staying on track.
2. Celebrate your successes: Celebrate your financial successes, no matter how small, to keep yourself motivated.
3. Be flexible: Be willing to make adjustments to your budget and financial plan as needed.
4. Surround yourself with support: Surround yourself with supportive people who will encourage you and hold you accountable.
5. Stay informed: Stay informed about personal finance and budgeting by reading books, attending workshops, and seeking the advice of financial professionals.

Staying on track with your personal finance goals requires discipline, commitment, and a little extra effort. By following the steps outlined in this chapter, you'll be able to stay focused on your financial goals and achieve financial stability and success. In the next chapter, we'll summarize the key takeaways from this book and offer some final thoughts.

Chapter VIII: Final Thoughts

In this chapter, we'll summarize the key takeaways from this book and offer some final thoughts on personal finance and budgeting.

Here are the key takeaways from this book:
1. Personal finance is the process of managing your money to achieve financial stability, security, and independence.
2. Setting financial goals is an essential part of personal finance that provides direction and motivation for your financial journey.
3. A budget is a financial plan that helps you manage your money by tracking your income and expenses.
4. Saving and investing are critical components of personal finance that help you build wealth and achieve financial security.
5. Managing debt is important for achieving financial stability and reducing financial stress.
6. Protecting your finances means taking steps to safeguard your money, assets, and personal information from theft, fraud, and other financial threats.
7. Staying on track with your personal finance goals requires discipline, commitment, and a little extra effort.

By following the guidelines outlined in this book, you'll be able to take control of your finances, achieve your financial goals, and build a brighter financial future. Personal finance and budgeting may seem overwhelming, but with the right approach and a little effort, you can master these essential skills and achieve financial success.

XI: Additional Topics

Understanding Interest Rates and Compound Interest

Here's a closer look at interest rates and compound interest:

1. Interest Rates: An interest rate is the amount charged by a lender to a borrower for the use of money. Interest rates can be fixed or variable and can have a significant impact on the cost of borrowing.

2. Compound Interest: Compound interest is the interest that is calculated not only on the original principal, but also on the accumulated interest from previous periods. Compound interest can have a significant impact on the growth of your savings and investments.

3. The Benefits of Understanding Interest Rates and Compound Interest: By understanding interest rates and compound interest, you can make informed decisions about borrowing and investing and achieve your financial goals.

The Benefits of Automated Savings and Investment

Here are some benefits of automated savings and investment:

1. Consistency: Automated savings and investment ensure that you are saving and investing regularly, even when life gets busy.
2. Convenience: Automated savings and investment take the effort and discipline out of saving and investing, making it easier to reach your financial goals.
3. Avoiding Procrastination: Automated savings and investment help you avoid procrastination and the tendency to delay saving and investing.
4. Dollar Cost Averaging: Automated investment can help you take advantage of dollar cost averaging, which is a strategy for investing a set amount of money at regular intervals, regardless of market conditions.
5. Achieving Your Goals Faster: Automated savings and investment can help you reach your financial goals faster and with less effort.

By implementing automated savings and investment strategies, you can improve your financial situation and achieve your financial goals faster and with less effort. In the next chapter, we'll focus on the benefits of living below your means, which is an important component of personal finance.

The Pros and Cons of Renting vs. Owning a Home

Here's a closer look at the pros and cons of renting vs. owning a home:

Pros of Renting:
1. Flexibility: Renting offers greater flexibility, allowing you to move easily if your job or lifestyle changes.
2. Lower Upfront Costs: Renting requires a lower upfront cost than buying a home, making it a more affordable option for many people.
3. No Maintenance Costs: As a renter, you don't have to worry about maintenance costs or repairs, which can be a significant advantage.

Cons of Renting:
1. Lack of Equity: Renting does not build equity, meaning you don't own any part of the property you're renting.
2. Limited Control: As a renter, you have limited control over the property and may not be able to make changes or renovations.

Pros of Owning a Home:
1. Building Equity: Owning a home allows you to build equity, which can be a valuable asset in the future.
2. Potential Appreciation: Owning a home can result in potential appreciation, meaning the value of the property may increase over time.
3. Tax Benefits: Owning a home can result in tax benefits, such as the mortgage interest tax deduction.

Cons of Owning a Home:
1. Higher Upfront Costs: Buying a home requires a higher upfront cost, including a down payment and closing costs.
2. Maintenance Costs: Owning a home comes with maintenance costs, including repairs and renovations.

By understanding the pros and cons of renting vs. owning a home, you can make an informed decision about which option is best for you and your financial situation. In the next chapter, we'll focus on understanding the stock market and investing in stocks, which is an important component of personal finance.

How to Save for Retirement

Here are some tips for saving for retirement:

1. Start early: The earlier you start saving for retirement, the more time your savings will have to grow.
2. Make it a priority: Make saving for retirement a priority and allocate a portion of your income to this goal.
3. Take advantage of tax-advantaged accounts: Consider using tax-advantaged accounts, such as a 401(k) or IRA, to save for retirement.
4. Increase your contributions: Increase your contributions over time as your income and financial situation improve.
5. Consider professional advice: Consider seeking professional advice from a financial advisor to help you save for retirement effectively.

By following these tips, you can ensure a comfortable future and avoid financial stress in your golden years. In the next chapter, we'll focus on understanding the different types of insurance, which is an important component of personal finance.

How to Build and Maintain Good Credit

Here are some tips for building and maintaining good credit:

1. Pay your bills on time: Paying your bills on time is the most important factor in building and maintaining good credit.
2. Keep your credit utilization low: Keep your credit utilization, or the amount of credit you're using compared to your credit limit, low to maintain good credit.
3. Monitor your credit report: Regularly monitor your credit report to catch any errors or signs of fraud and address them promptly.
4. Limit new credit applications: Limit the number of new credit applications, as frequent applications can have a negative impact on your credit score.
5. Use a mix of credit types: Use a mix of credit types, such as credit cards and loans, to demonstrate responsible credit management.

By following these tips, you can build and maintain good credit, which is an important aspect of personal finance. In the next chapter, we'll focus on how to save for a big purchase, which is an important component of personal finance.

Understanding the Different Types of Insurance

Here are some of the different types of insurance:

1. Health Insurance: Health insurance covers the cost of medical treatment and can help protect you from financial loss due to unexpected health events.
2. Life Insurance: Life insurance provides financial support to your loved ones in the event of your death.
3. Homeowner's Insurance: Homeowner's insurance covers the cost of repairing or rebuilding your home in the event of damage or loss.
4. Auto Insurance: Auto insurance covers the cost of repairing or replacing your vehicle in the event of damage or loss.
5. Disability Insurance: Disability insurance provides financial support in the event of a disability that prevents you from working.

When choosing insurance, it's important to consider your specific needs and budget. You may need to purchase multiple types of insurance to fully protect yourself and your assets. In the next chapter, we'll focus on understanding the benefits of living below your means, which is an important component of personal finance.

How to Save for a Big Purchase

Here are some tips for saving for a big purchase:

1. Set a goal: Set a goal for the amount you want to save and a deadline for reaching this goal.
2. Create a budget: Create a budget that includes saving for your big purchase and stick to it.
3. Automate your savings: Automate your savings by setting up automatic transfers from your checking account to your savings account.
4. Avoid impulse purchases: Avoid impulse purchases and stick to your budget to reach your savings goal faster.
5. Consider a side hustle: Consider earning extra income through a side hustle to increase your savings and reach your goal faster.

By following these tips, you can save for a big purchase effectively and improve your financial situation. In the next chapter, we'll focus on creating a financial plan for the future, which is an important component of personal finance.

Understanding the Benefits of Living Below Your Means

Living below your means is a lifestyle choice that can have numerous benefits for your financial stability and overall well-being. Here are some of the key advantages of living below your means:

1. Increased Savings: When you live below your means, you are able to save a larger portion of your income, which can help you build up your emergency fund and plan for your future financial goals.

2. Reduced Debt: By spending less money than you earn, you are less likely to accumulate debt and more likely to pay off existing debts faster.

3. Increased Financial Flexibility: When you have a lower monthly burn rate, you have more financial flexibility to handle unexpected expenses, such as medical bills, car repairs, or job loss.

4. Improved Mental Health: Living below your means can reduce stress and anxiety related to financial issues. It allows you to focus on what truly matters in life, rather than constantly worrying about money.

5. Better Budgeting Habits: When you live below your means, you are more mindful of your spending and develop better budgeting habits. This can help you make informed financial decisions and avoid impulsive purchases.

6. Increased Financial Independence: By living below your means and saving a significant portion of your income, you can become financially independent and reduce your dependence on others for financial support.

In conclusion, living below your means is a smart financial strategy that can provide numerous benefits for your financial stability and well-being. By prioritizing savings and reducing unnecessary spending, you can achieve financial independence and live a more fulfilling life.

Creating a financial plan for the future can help you achieve your financial goals and ensure that you are on track to a secure financial future. Here are the steps to create a financial plan:

1. Define your financial goals: Before you create a financial plan, it's important to determine what you want to achieve. Do you want to save for retirement, pay off debt, or build an emergency fund? Be specific and set achievable goals.

2. Assess your current financial situation: Take an inventory of your current assets, liabilities, and income. This will give you a good understanding of where you stand financially and help you identify areas for improvement.

3. Create a budget: A budget will help you track your spending and identify areas where you can reduce costs. It's important to stick to your budget as closely as possible to ensure that you stay on track with your financial goals.

4. Start saving: Make saving a priority in your budget. Establish an emergency fund, and contribute to a retirement account such as a 401(k) or IRA. Automate your savings so that you don't have to think about it.

5. Invest wisely: Consider investing a portion of your savings in a diversified portfolio of low-cost index funds. This can help you grow your wealth over time and achieve your long-term financial goals.

6. Re-evaluate your plan regularly: Your financial situation and goals may change over time, so it's important to re-evaluate your plan regularly and make adjustments as needed.

By following these steps and sticking to your financial plan, you can achieve your financial goals and secure your financial future. Remember that building wealth takes time and discipline, so it's important to stay focused and committed to your plan.

We hope that this book has been helpful in providing you with the knowledge and tools you need to take control of your finances and achieve your financial goals. Remember, personal finance is a lifelong journey and requires ongoing effort and discipline.

Thank you for reading and we wish you the best of luck on your personal finance journey.

BINXOM

www.ingramcontent.com/pod-product-compliance
Lightning Source LLC
Chambersburg PA
CBHW072151230526

45467CB00042B/1668

9 7 9 8 3 7 9 0 7 5 7 6 7